CW00558476

BRANCH LINES AROUND HERTFORD AND HATFIELD

Vic Mitchell and Keith Smith

MP Middleton Press

Front cover: The fine tracery on the canopy stanchion at Hertford East frames class L1 2-6-4T no. 67718 as it arrives with the 2.58pm from Broxbourne on 2nd June 1956. (H.C.Casserley)

Rear cover: Standing at Hertford East on 21st May 1995 is EMU no. 317392 waiting to depart for Broxbourne at 16.10. The centre track has since been lifted. (H.Ballantyne)

Published August 2009

ISBN 978 1 906008 58 1

© Middleton Press, 2009

Design Deborah Esher
Typesetting Barbara Mitchell

Published by
>   *Middleton Press*
>   *Easebourne Lane*
>   *Midhurst*
>   *West Sussex*
>   *GU29 9AZ*
Tel: 01730 813169
Fax: 01730 812601
Email: info@middletonpress.co.uk
www.middletonpress.co.uk

Printed in the United Kingdom by Henry Ling Limited, at the Dorset Press, Dorchester, DT1 1HD

CONTENTS

INDEX

ACKNOWLEDGEMENTS

We are very grateful for the assistance received from many of those mentioned in the credits, also to B.Bennett, A.R.Carder, L.Crosier, G.Croughton, J.B.Horne, S.C.Jenkins, N.Langridge, B.Lewis, D.H.Mitchell, B.I.Nathan, R.Price, Mr D. and Dr S.Salter, M.Turvey, T.Walsh and in particular, our always supportive wives, Barbara Mitchell and Janet Smith.

I. 1947 Railway Clearing House diagram, devoid of halts.

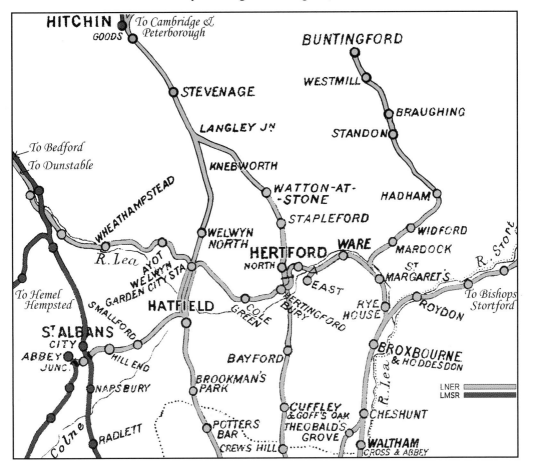

GEOGRAPHICAL SETTING

Hertford is the county town of Hertfordshire and all the routes are within that county. The area is situated on the gentle dip slope of the chalk of the northern extension of the Chiltern Hills.

The route from Broxbourne to Hertford follows up the curving valley of the River Lea. Trains westwards ran close to it and passed over it north of Hatfield. At St. Albans, the valley of the River Ver is reached. The Buntingford branch follows the River Ash for its first four miles, passes over a watershed and enters the valley of the River Rib for the final four miles.

The maps are to the scale of 25ins to 1 mile, with north at the top, unless otherwise indicated.

Branch gradient profile

HISTORICAL BACKGROUND

The first line to Hertford was from the east and was opened by the Northern & Eastern Railway on 31st October 1843 as a branch from its 1840 main line at Broxbourne. The branch was authorised by an Act of 21st June 1841. The N&ER was leased to the Eastern Counties Railway on 1st January 1844.

Trains came to Hertford from the west on 1st March 1858 on a branch from the Great Northern Railway's 1850 main line at Welwyn Junction. The route was built by the Hertford & Welwyn Junction Railway under an Act of 3rd July 1854. It became part of the Hertford, Luton & Dunstable Railway which formed a constituent of the GNR in 1861. All trains ran from Hatfield or beyond, on both this branch and the next to be described.

The Hatfield & St. Albans Railway came into use on 16th October 1865, having been built under an Act of 30th June 1862. It became part of the GNR in 1883. The London & North Western Railway had opened a branch from Watford to St. Albans on 5th May 1858.

The N&ER was built to 5ft gauge and was relaid to 4ft 8½ ins in 1844. It became part of the Great Eastern Railway on 7th August 1862. The Midland Railway's main line was opened through St. Albans in 1867.

The GNR completed a relief line between Stevenage and Enfield for goods in 1918 and a passenger station for Hertford was opened on it on 2nd June 1924. It was known as "North". The GNR and GER had become part of the new London & North Eastern Railway in 1923. This largely formed the Eastern Region of British Railways upon nationalisation in 1948. The story of the various stations in Hertford is told in detail in that section of this volume.

Closures began on 1st October 1951, when passenger service was curtailed between Hertford and St. Albans. Goods facilities were withdrawn at most locations on the route in 1965-68. Details are in the captions.

Full electric services on the Hertford East line began on 21st November 1960, the current being 25kV AC. The same applied at Hertford North from 8th November 1976, but only southwards. Electric services northwards began on 6th February 1978.

Buntingford Branch

The line was built under the provisions of an Act dated 12th July 1858 by the Ware, Hadham & Buntingford Railway. It opened on 3rd July 1863 and became part of the GER on 30th July 1868. Passenger service was withdrawn on 16th November 1964 and goods followed on 20th September 1965.

Privatisation

West Anglia Great Northern or WAGN was that part of Prism Rail which received a 7¼ year franchise from 5th January 1997. Under the title of 'One', there was an extension until March 2007. Subsequently services to Hertford East have been operated by National Express East Anglia.

PASSENGER SERVICES

The frequency of down trains in the early years of four branches is shown to indicate the differing development of services.

	Broxbourne to Hertford		Hertford to Hatfield		Hatfield to St. Albans		St. Margaret's to Buntingford	
	Weekdays	Sundays	Weekdays	Sundays	Weekdays	Sundays	Weekdays	Sundays
1869	9	4	7	2	10	2	4	2
1889	22	5	10	2	11	2	6	2
1909	22	7	12	3	11	2	8	2
1929	25	12	8	0	8	0	10	3

The final timetable for the Buntingford branch had nine trains, but peak hours only. The Sunday service had been withdrawn in 1955. The last timetable to St. Albans comprised just one train, Mondays to Fridays only. The final trains west from Hertford numbered six, weekdays only.

The Hertford East line was the reverse of the others and improved steadily. Since electrification it has had an excellent 30-minute interval basic service, with more at peak times.

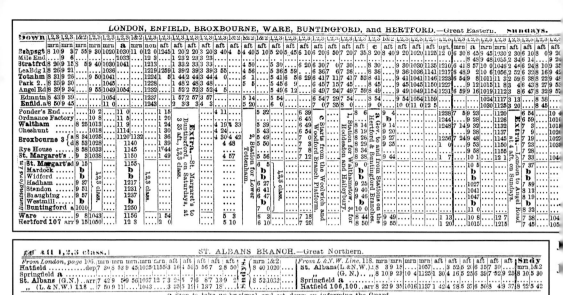

LONDON, ENFIELD, BROXBOURNE, WARE, BUNTINGFORD, and HERTFORD.—Great Eastern. Sundays.

a Stop to take up by signal, and set down on informing the Guard.

ST. ALBANS BRANCH.—Great Northern.

From London, page 106.

FARES.—London to St. Albans, 1st class, 3s. 6d.; 2nd, 2s. 6d.; 3rd, 1s. 11½d. RETURN TICKETS, 5s. 6d.; 4s. Passengers can be booked between St. Albans (G.N. and L. & N.W. Stations), fares, 4d.; 3d.; 2d. Passengers are also booked through between Hertford and Hatfield and Rickmansworth, Watford, and Bushey, via St. Albans.

HATFIELD and HERTFORD.—Great Northern.

March 190

x Through Train to Hertford. ¶ Cowbridge Station; ½ mile to Great Eastern Station, and 2½ miles to Haileybury College.

HATFIELD and ST. ALBANS.—Great Northern.

March 190

BUNTINGFORD and ST. MARGARET'S.—Great Eastern.

March 190

HATFIELD and HERTFORD NORTH.

A Arr. at 7 10 aft. on Sats. B Dep. at 7 5 aft. on Fris. E Except Sats. L ½ mile to East Station and 2½ miles to Haileybury College. S Sats. only.

BUNTINGFORD AND ST. MARGARET'S.

July 1929

NOTES.
D Station for Stanstead Abbots.
E Except Saturdays.
S Saturdays only.

ST. MARGARET'S and BUNTINGFORD Ⓐ Third class only Ⓐ

July 1949

Miles		Week Days a.m	a.m	a.m	a.m E	a.m S		p.m S	p.m	p.m EZ	p.m S	p.m E	p.m E		p.m EZ	p.m S	p.m S	p.m E		Sundays. a.m		p.m	p.m
	Liverpool St., 9 London .... dep	5Z50	6Z56	8 28	1040	1042	..	1 30	2Z25	4 15	4 25	4 54	5 27	..	6 5	6 7	8Z22	8Z22	..	8Z20	..	6 40	8 5
—	St. Margaret's ...... dep	7 8	7 53	9 41	1154	1154	..	2 18	3 14	5 6	5 33	5 55	6 27	..	6 51	7 10	9 14	9 22	..	9 6	..	7 27	9 15
2¾	Mardock	7 14	7 59	9 47	12 0	12 0	..	2 24	3 20	5 12	5 39	6 1	6 33	..	6 57	7 16	9 20	9 28	..	9 12	..	7 33	9 21
3¾	Widford	7 17	8 2	9 50	12 3	12 3	..	2 27	3 23	5 15	5 42	6 5	6 36	..	7 0	7 19	9 23	9 31	..	9 15	..	7 36	9 24
5¾	Hadham	7 26	8 8	9 57	12 9	12 9	..	2 33	3 29	5 22	5 48	6 10	6 42	..	7 7	7 25	9 29	9 37	..	9 21	..	7 42	9 30
9¼	Standon	7 34	8 16	10 5	1217	1217	..	2 41	3 37	5 30	5 56	6 18	6 50	..	7 14	7 33	9 37	9 45	..	9 29	..	7 50	9 38
10¾	Braughing	7 37	8 22	10 8	1221	1221	..	2 45	3 41	5 33	6 0	6 21	6 53	..	7 17	7 37	9 41	9 49	..	9 32	..	7 53	9 41
12¼	West Mill	7 42	8 27	1013	1226	1226	..	2 50	3 46	5 38	6 5	6 26	6 58	..	7 22	7 42	9 46	9 54	..	9 37	..	7 58	9 46
13¾	Buntingford .... arr	7 46	8 31	1017	1230	1230	..	2 54	3 50	5 42	6 9	6 30	7 2	..	7 26	7 45	9 50	9 58	..	9 41	..	8 2	9 50

Miles		Week Days a.m	a.m	a.m EZ	a.m S	a.m EZ	a.m S	a.m	a.m E	a.m S	p.m S	p.m E	p.m S	p.m E	p.m S	p.m E	p.m E	p.m S	p.m E	Sundays. a.m		p.m F	p.m
—	Buntingford .... dep	6 11	7 4	8 10	8 13	8 57	8 57	9 35	1051	11 0	1249	1 37	4 1	4 59	6 20	6 43	7 57	8 22	9 15	7 25	..	6 28	8 15
1¼	West Mill	6 14	7 7	8 13	8 16	9 0	9 0	9 38	1054	11 3	1252	1 40	4 4	5 2	6 23	6 47	8 0	8 25	9 18	7 28	..	6 31	8 18
3¼	Braughing	6 20	7 12	8 19	8 21	9 5	9 5	9 43	11 0	11 8	1257	1 45	4 9	5 7	6 28	6 54	8 5	8 30	9 23	7 33	..	6 36	8 23
4½	Standon	6 23	7 15	8 22	8 24	9 8	9 8	9 46	11 3	1111	1 0	1 48	4 12	5 11	6 31	6 57	8 8	8 33	9 26	7 36	..	6 39	8 26
8	Hadham	6 31	7 24	8 30	8 32	9 16	9 16	9 56	1112	1119	1 8	1 56	4 20	5 22	6 39	7 6	8 18	8 41	9 38	7 44	..	6 47	8 34
10	Widford	6 36	7 29	8 35	8 37	9 21	9 21	10 1	1117	1124	1 13	2 1	4 25	5 27	6 44	7 11	8 23	8 46	9 43	7 49	..	6 52	8 39
11	Mardock	6 39	7 32	8 38	8 40	9 24	9 24	10 4	1121	1127	1 16	2 4	4 28	5 30	6 47	7 14	8 26	8 49	9 46	7 52	..	6 55	8 42
13¾	St. Margaret's A .. arr	6 45	7 38	8 44	8 46	9 30	9 30	1010	1127	1133	1 22	2 10	4 34	5 36	6 53	7 20	8 32	8 55	9 52	7 58	..	7 1	8 48
32¾	9 London (L. St.) .. arr	7 40	8 40	9 32	9 32	1025	1030	1121	1227	1239	2 28	3 20	5 40	6 44	7 58	8C33	9 39	10 1	1059	8Z55	..	7 52	9 58

A Station for Stanstead Abbott's. **C** Change at Stratford. **D** Does not run after 11th September.
E Except Saturdays. **F** Through Train between Buntingford and Liverpool Street until 11th September.
S Saturdays only. **Z** Through Train between Liverpool Street and Buntingford.
Z First and Third class between Liverpool Street and Broxbourne.

HATFIELD and ST. ALBANS
Third class only, except where otherwise shown

July 1949

Miles		Week Days only E		S	F		J		
	8 London (King's C.) dep	7 18	..	12p25	4Ap10	..	5Ap10	..	..
—	Hatfield .... dep	8 10	..	1 7	5 8	.	5 50	..	..
2	Nast Hyde Halt.........	8 15	..	1 14	5 18	..	6 18	..	..
2¾	Smallford for Colney	8 18	..	1 17	5 21	..	6 21	..	..
4	Hill End ....[Heath	8 23	..	1 22	5 26	..	6 26	..	..
5½	St. Albans (E.R.) arr	8 28	..	1 27	5 31	..	6 31	..	..
	St. Albans (E.R.) dep	8 29	..	1 28	5 32	..	6 32	..	..
6½	" (Abbey) L... arr	8 32	..	1 31	5 35	..	6 35	..	..

Miles		Week Days only S	E		F	J	
	St. Albans (Abbey) L dep	7 5	7 28	..	4p29	5p5	..
¾	" (E.R.) arr	7 7	7 31	..	4 32	5 8	..
	" (E.R.) dep	7 9	7 32	..	4 33	5 9	..
2¼	Hill End ......[Heath..	7 14	7 37	..	4 41	5 14	..
3½	Smallford, for Colney	7 18	7 41	..	4 45	5 18	..
4½	Nast Hyde Halt.........	7 21	7 44	..	4 48	5 21	..
6½	Hatfield .... arr	7 29	7 52	..	4 54	5 27	..
24½	8 London (King's C.) arr	8 13	8C43	..	5 55	6 31	..

A First and Third class between London (King's Cross) and Hatfield. **C** Arr. 8 48 a.m. on Saturdays. **E** Except Saturdays
F Fridays only **J** Except Fridays and Saturdays. **L** L.M.R. *p* p.m. **S** Saturdays only.

WELWYN GARDEN CITY and HERTFORD (North)
Third class only, except where otherwise shown

July 1949

Miles		Week Days a.m		a.m	Sats. only a.m		Sats. only p.m		p.m	Except Saturdays p.m	Sats. only p.m	Except Saturdays p.m		Sundays			
	8 London (King's C.) dep	..	..	7 18	10B40	..	12B15	..	4B22	5B34	5B34	..	..	..	..	..	..
	8 Hatfield .... "	..	..	8 20	11B12	..	12 48	..	4 56	5 55	6 17	6 17	..	..	..	..	..
—	Welwyn Garden City..	5 57	..	8 35	11 27	..	12 58	..	5 12	6 12	6 40	6 40	..	..	..	..	..
4	Cole Green..............	6 6	..	8 44	11 36	..	1 7	..	5 21	6 21	6 49	6 49	..	..	..	..	..
5½	Hertingfordbury	6 11	..	8 49	11 41	..	1 12	..	5 26	6 26	6 54	6 54	..	..	..	..	..
6½	Hertford (North)... arr	6 17	..	8 54	11 47	..	1 16	..	5 30	6 30	6 58	6 58	..	..	..	..	..

Miles		Week Days a.m	a.m	a.m	Sats. only p.m	Sats. only p.m	Except Saturdays p.m	Sats. only p.m	Except Saturdays p.m	Sats. only p.m	Sats. only p.m	Except Saturdays p.m	Sundays			
	Hertford (North)...dep	7 10	7 28	9 15	12 2	1 35	4 10	4 10	5 45	5 45	7 18	7 18	..	..	..	..
1	Hertingfordbury	7 14	7 32	9 19	12 6	1 39	4 14	4 14	5 49	5 49	7 22	7 22	..	..	..	..
2½	Cole Green..............	7 20	7 38	9 25	1212	1 45	4 20	4 20	5 55	5 55	7 28	7 28	..	..	..	..
6½	Welwyn Garden City..	7 27	7 45	9 32	1219	1 52	4 27	4 27	6 2	6 2	7 35	7 35	..	..	..	..
9	8 Hatfield .... arr	7 36	7 55	9B41	1226	2 5	4 43	4 40	6 25	6 25	7 48	7 52	..	..	..	..
26¾	8 London (King's C.) "	8 13	8B22	10B12	1 13	2B50	5 13	5 30	6B52	7 17	8 32	8B40	..	..	..	..

B First and Third class between London (King's Cross) and Welwyn Garden City.

Table 10 ST. MARGARET'S and BUNTINGFORD Ⓐ Third class only Ⓐ

September 1950

Miles		Week Days a.m	a.m	a.m	a.m E	p.m S	p.m S	p.m S	p.m E	p.m S	p.m EZ	p.m S	p.m E	p.m E	p.m EZ	p.m S	p.m S	p.m E		Sundays a.m		p.m	p.m
	Liverpool St., 9 London .... dep	5Z50	6 37	8 28	1040	1044	1235	1 30	2Z25	2Z25	4 15	4 25	4 54	5 27	6 0	6 7	8Z22	8Z22	..	8Z20	..	6 40	8 15
—	St. Margaret's ...... dep	7 8	7 47	9 41	1152	1154	1 38	2 18	3 14	3 16	5 6	5 33	5 55	6 27	6 49	7 10	9 14	9 18	..	9 6	..	7 27	9 17
2¾	Mardock	7 14	7 53	9 47	1158	12 0	1 44	2 24	3 20	3 22	5 12	5 39	6 1	6 33	6 55	7 16	9 20	9 24	..	9 12	..	7 33	9 23
3¾	Widford	7 17	7 56	9 50	12 1	12 3	1 47	2 27	3 23	3 25	5 15	5 42	6 5	6 36	6 58	7 19	9 23	9 27	..	9 15	..	7 36	9 26
5¾	Hadham	7 26	8 2	9 57	12 7	12 9	1 53	2 33	3 29	3 31	5 22	5 48	6 10	6 42	7 5	7 25	9 29	9 36	..	9 21	..	7 42	9 32
9¼	Standon	7 34	8 10	10 5	1215	1217	2 1	2 41	3 37	3 39	5 30	5 56	6 18	6 50	7 12	7 33	9 37	9 44	..	9 29	..	7 50	9 40
10¾	Braughing	7 37	8U22	10 8	1219	1221	2 4	2 45	3 41	3 43	5 33	6 0	6 21	6 53	7 15	7 37	9 41	9 48	..	9 32	..	7 53	9 43
12¼	West Mill	7 42	8 27	1013	1224	1226	2 9	2 50	3 46	3 48	5 38	6 5	6 26	6 58	7 20	7 42	9 46	9 53	..	9 37	..	7 58	9 48
13¾	Buntingford .... arr	7 46	8 31	1017	1228	1230	2 13	2 54	3 50	3 52	5 42	6 8	6 30	7 2	7 24	7 45	9 50	9 57	..	9 41	..	8 2	9 52

Miles		Week Days a.m	a.m	a.m EZ	a.m S	a.m EZ	a.m S	a.m	a.m E	a.m S	p.m S	p.m E	p.m S	p.m S	p.m E	p.m S	p.m E	p.m E	p.m S	p.m E	Sundays a.m	p.m	p.m
—	Buntingford .... dep	6 11	7 4	8 10	8 13	8 57	8 57	9 35	1051	11 0	1249	1 37	2 35	4 1	4 59	6 20	6 43	7 57	8 22	9 15	7 25	6 28	8 15
1¼	West Mill	6 14	7 7	8 13	8 16	9 0	9 0	9 38	1054	11 3	1252	1 40	2 38	4 4	5 2	6 23	6 47	8 0	8 25	9 18	7 28	6 31	8 18
3¼	Braughing	6 20	7 12	8 19	8 21	9 5	9 5	9 43	11 0	11 8	1257	1 45	2 44	4 9	5 7	6 28	6 54	8 5	8 30	9 23	7 33	6 36	8 23
4½	Standon	6 23	7 15	8 22	8 24	9 8	9 8	9 46	11 3	1111	1 0	1 48	2 47	4 12	5 11	6 31	6 57	8 8	8 33	9 26	7 36	6 39	8 26
8	Hadham	6 31	7 24	8 30	8 32	9 16	9 16	9 56	1112	1119	1 8	1 56	2 55	4 20	5 22	6 39	7 6	8 18	8 41	9 34	7 44	6 47	8 34
10	Widford	6 36	7 29	8 35	8 37	9 21	9 21	10 1	1117	1124	1 13	2 1	3 0	4 25	5 27	6 44	7 11	8 23	8 46	9 39	7 49	6 52	8 39
11	Mardock	6 39	7 32	8 38	8 40	9 24	9 24	10 4	1121	1127	1 16	2 4	3 3	4 28	5 30	6 47	7 14	8 26	8 49	9 42	7 52	6 55	8 42
13¾	St. Margaret's A .. arr	6 45	7 38	8 44	8 46	9 30	9 30	1010	1127	1133	1 22	2 10	3 9	4 34	5 36	6 53	7 20	8 32	8 55	9 48	7 58	7 1	8 48
32¾	9 London (L. St.) .. arr	7 41	8 40	9 32	9 32	1026	1030	1121	1227	1239	2 28	3 20	4 12	5 40	6 44	7 58	8C33	9 39	10 1	1059	8Z55	7 52	9 55

A Station for Stanstead Abbott's. **C** Change at Stratford. **E** Except Saturdays. **S** Saturdays only. **U** Arr 8 12 a.m.
Z Through Train between Liverpool St. and Buntingford Z First and Third class between Liverpool St. and Broxbourne

HATFIELD and ST. ALBANS
Third class only, except where otherwise shown

September 1951

Miles		Week Days only p.m. F		p.m. J					
	8 London (King's C.) dep	4A21	..	5A10	..	..	..	..	..
—	Hatfield .... dep	5 8	..	5 50	..	..	..	..	..
2	Nast Hyde Halt.........	5 18	..	6 18	..	..	..	..	..
2¾	Smallford, for Colney	5 21	..	6 21	..	..	..	..	..
4	Hill End ....[Heath	5 26	..	6 26	..	..	..	..	..
5½	St. Albans (E.R.) arr	5 31	..	6 31	..	..	..	..	..
	St. Albans (E.R.) dep	5 32	..	6 32	..	..	..	..	..
6½	" (Abbey) L... arr	5 35	..	6 35	..	..	..	..	..

Miles		Week Days only a.m E					
	St. Albans (Abbey) L dep	7 28	..	..	..	..	..
¾	" (E.R.) arr	7 31	..	..	..	..	..
	" (E.R.) dep	7 32	..	..	..	..	..
2¼	Hill End ......[Heath..	7 37	..	..	..	..	..
3½	Smallford, for Colney	7 41	..	..	..	..	..
4½	Nast Hyde Halt.........	7 44	..	..	..	..	..
6½	Hatfield .... arr	7 52	..	..	..	..	..
24½	8 London (King's C.) arr	8n43	..	..	..	..	..

A First and Third class London (King's Cross) to Hatfield. **E** Except Saturdays **F** Fridays only
J Except Fridays and Saturdays. **L** L.M.R. *n* Change at Finsbury Park.

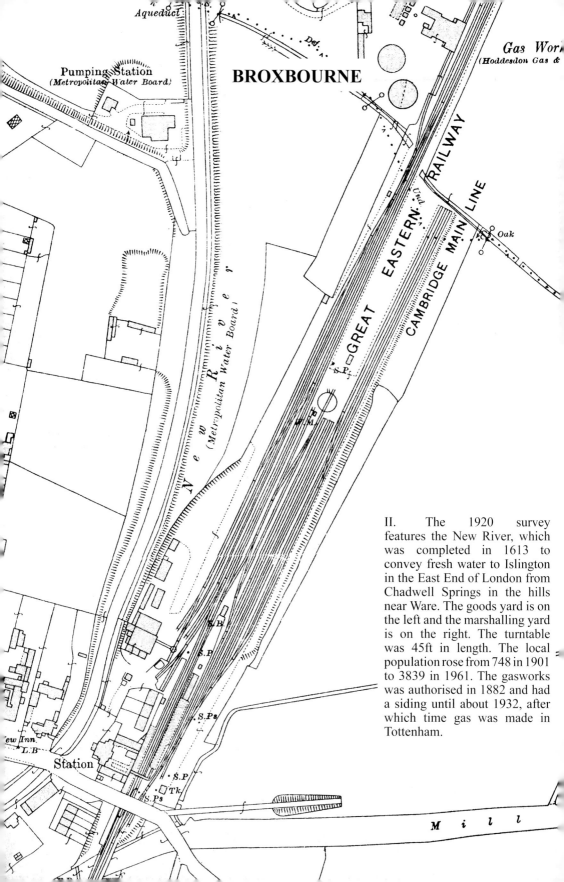

Aqueduct

Pumping Station
(Metropolitan Water Board)

BROXBOURNE

Gas Wor
(Hoddesdon Gas &

RAILWAY

GREAT EASTERN

CAMBRIDGE MAIN LINE

Oak

River
(Metropolitan Water Board)

New

ew Inn
L.B

Station

S.P
Tk
S.Ps

M i l l

II. The 1920 survey features the New River, which was completed in 1613 to convey fresh water to Islington in the East End of London from Chadwell Springs in the hills near Ware. The goods yard is on the left and the marshalling yard is on the right. The turntable was 45ft in length. The local population rose from 748 in 1901 to 3839 in 1961. The gasworks was authorised in 1882 and had a siding until about 1932, after which time gas was made in Tottenham.

1.   A postcard view from the bridge over the New River in about 1900 includes a perambulator and an omnibus of the period, plus staff cottages and the long roof over the footbridge. Six cottages had been built in 1847; they lasted until 1979. (SLS coll.)

2.   More of the footbridge is to be seen on 2nd June 1956 as 0-6-2T no. 69723 called with the 3.0pm Stratford to Hertford East train. On the right is the dock for the horse-drawn coaches of the gentry. (H.C.Casserley)

3.   A northward panorama in 1955 includes the busy goods yard on the left, together with a terminating passenger train. Shunting is in progress on the right. In the left background is Hoddesdon Gasworks and on the right is Rye House Power Station. (Lens of Sutton coll.)

L. N. E. R.
CHILD

8381

FOR CONDITIONS SEE BACK. Available for three days, including day of issue.

RYE HOUSE to

BROXBOURNE & HODDESDON

Third Class Fare 2½dP

8381

L. & N. E. R.

Not transferable Issued subject to Regulations in the Company's Time Tables

RYE HOUSE to

Rye House   Rye House

HERTFORD EAST

Hertford E   Hertford E

7½d   FARE   7½d

THIRD CLASS

Available on day of issue only

4.	A 1956 northward view reveals that the down platform had been extended under the road bridge and included is the water tank at the end of the up yard. (H.C.Casserley)

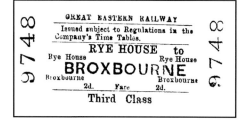

5.　　Class N7 0-6-2T no. 69677 runs in from the north and is close to the site of the temporary footbridge, which was used during the rebuilding in 1959-60. The new station was constructed immediately north of it. The 1932 65-lever signal box lasted until 10th July 1960. (R.S.Carpenter coll.)

6.　　Two of the four new platforms were recorded early in 1960, from the north. The new footbridge had a central wall to segregate passenger and parcel traffic. The official opening of the new station was on 3rd November 1960. (Lens of Sutton coll.)

7.   The car park on the left was laid out on the site of the old station and extended when the terrace of cottages (see map) was lost in 1979. Two island platforms were provided, which allowed fast trains to pass stopping ones. No. 31164 is setting back into the up yard on 8th June 1982 with sleepers from Costain's factory at Rye House. (R.Hummerston)

8.   The new signal box was built at the north end of the new up island platform and was in use until 27th May 2003, when it became an office and mess room for Network Rail. No. 315831 is working from Hertford East to Liverpool Street on 7th March 1985. (D.Pollock)

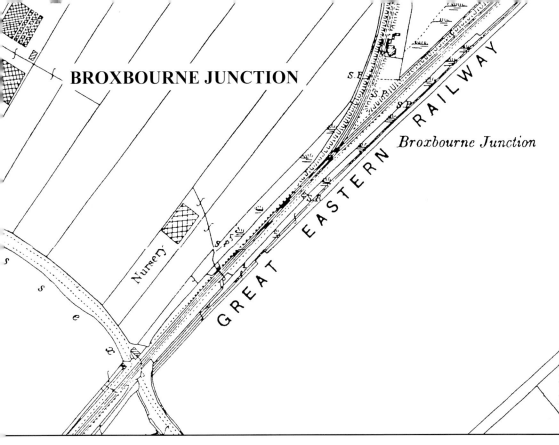

BROXBOURNE JUNCTION

Broxbourne Junction

III.   This is about one mile north of the station and is shown on the 1898 edition. At the bottom is Essex Road level crossing and its gatekeepers cottage. Rye House Power Station was built on the right of the main line in 1947 and was generating from 1951 to 1982, but was not demolished until 1992. Some of the sidings became an aggregate terminal.

9.   An undated view includes the junction signals and a main line train with probably a class L1 2-6-4T at its head. The branch had double track from 1846. Lifting barriers were fitted in 1980. The signal box was in use from 4th November 1951 to 31st January 1982 and was provided with a gate wheel, plus 35 levers. (A.Dudman coll.)

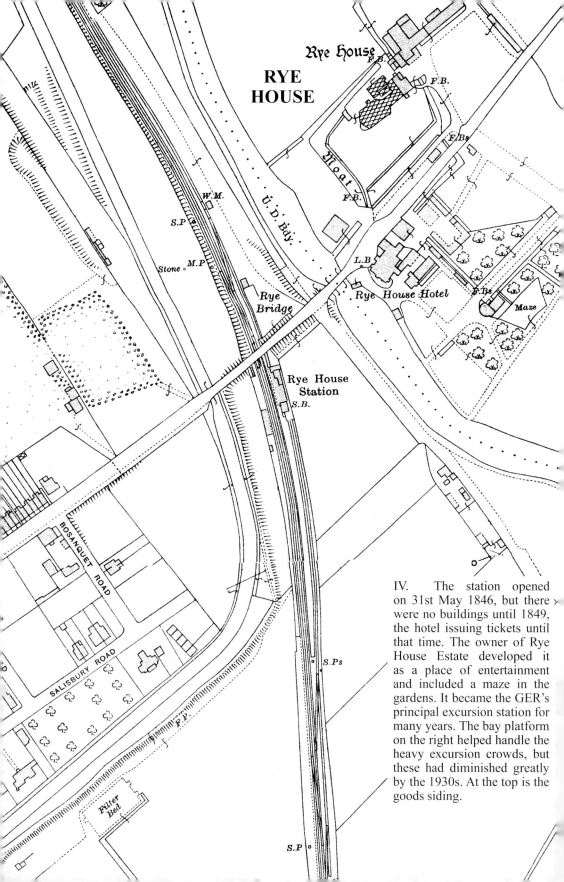

Rye House

RYE HOUSE

Moat

Rye House Hotel

F.Bs

Maze

L.B

U. D. Bdy.

W.M.

S.P

Stone M.P

Rye
Bridge

Rye House
Station

S.B.

BOSANQUET ROAD

SALISBURY ROAD

Filter
Bed

F.P

S.Ps

S.P

IV.   The station opened
on 31st May 1846, but there
were no buildings until 1849,
the hotel issuing tickets until
that time. The owner of Rye
House Estate developed it
as a place of entertainment
and included a maze in the
gardens. It became the GER's
principal excursion station for
many years. The bay platform
on the right helped handle the
heavy excursion crowds, but
these had diminished greatly
by the 1930s. At the top is the
goods siding.

10.　　The buildings lasted from 1871 until 1974, when simple shelters were provided. Seen in the mid-1950s, the bay was used for parcel traffic, which often included watercress. This was grown in the nearby spring water. Branching off the bay beyond the right border was a private siding to Costain's Concrete Works. Vast numbers of concrete sleepers were produced here and were despatched by rail until 1991. There was also a siding for Nissen Buildings Ltd from 1922 until after World War II. Their huts became famous during that conflict. (Views of Wells)

11.　　Beyond the bridge is the goods siding, which carried traffic until 31st January 1960. The 1885 signal box had 24 levers and closed on the same day. Further north was a siding for St. Margaret's Sand & Gravel Company and Hailey Brickworks in the 1920s. (Lens of Sutton coll.)

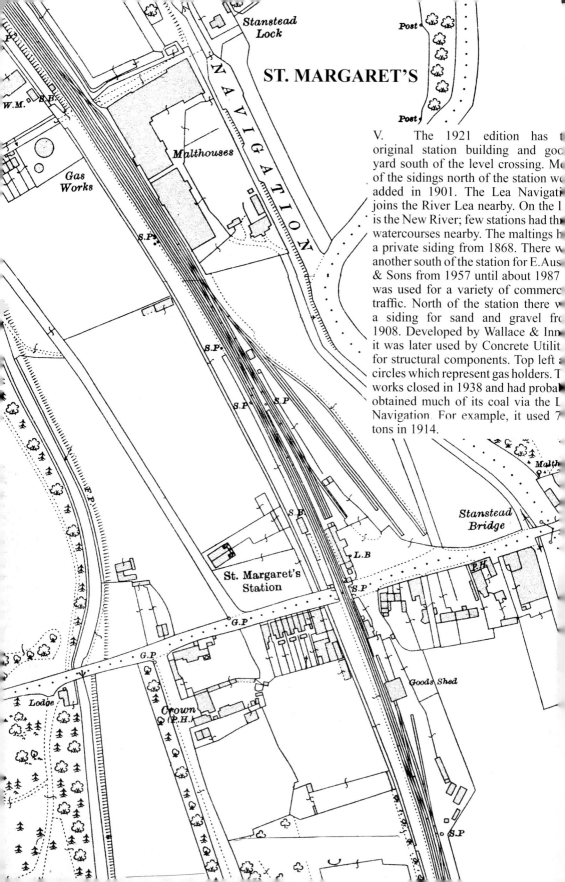

ST. MARGARET'S

V. The 1921 edition has t
original station building and goo
yard south of the level crossing. M
of the sidings north of the station w
added in 1901. The Lea Navigati
joins the River Lea nearby. On the l
is the New River; few stations had th
watercourses nearby. The maltings h
a private siding from 1868. There w
another south of the station for E.Aus
& Sons from 1957 until about 1987
was used for a variety of commerc
traffic. North of the station there w
a siding for sand and gravel fr
1908. Developed by Wallace & Inn
it was later used by Concrete Utilit
for structural components. Top left
circles which represent gas holders. T
works closed in 1938 and had proba
obtained much of its coal via the L
Navigation. For example, it used 7
tons in 1914.

12.   Two early postcards include the bay platform for Buntingford trains. It is in the centre background of this one and on the left of the next. The associated buildings were erected in 1863, when the branch opened. (Lens of Sutton coll.)

13.   The tall building beyond the 1887 signal initially served as the station, but after 1863 it became the house for the stationmaster. It was deemed appropriate to destroy it in June 1981. The up platform could take only five coaches, a limitation which still applied in 2005.
(Lens of Sutton coll.)

14.   A close-up of the bay in 1956 includes the suffix "and Stanstead Abbotts", plus the invitation to change for Buntingford. The locomotive is no. 69682, a class N7 0-6-2T. It has had to propel the branch coaches out of the platform before running round them. The 6-ton crane is near the centre. (H.C.Casserley)

15.   No. 69686 has just arrived with a train from Liverpool Street on 24th May 1958, as freshly painted no. 69633 waits with the connection to Buntingford. Both are class N7 0-6-2Ts. (D.K.Jones coll.)

16.   The panorama from a DMU in 1963 includes the almost redundant water tower and a new colour light signal. The goods yard was in use until 7th December 1970, but the branch passenger service had gone on 16th November 1964. The station was refurbished in 1986 and the adjacent land sold for housing. The journey to Buntingford continues at picture 91. (D.W.Sharp)

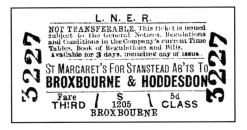

17.   The signalman controlled the level crossing gates, but, as he was so remote from them, conventional traffic lights were added, an unusual combination. Photographed on 5th May 1991, the relay room is on the right. (D.Pollock)

18.   The wheel-operated gates were changed to lifting barriers in 1969, but the 56-lever frame was retained. Only 11 of the levers were used in 1991. Closure came on 18th May 2003, when Liverpool Street took over the route. (D.Pollock)

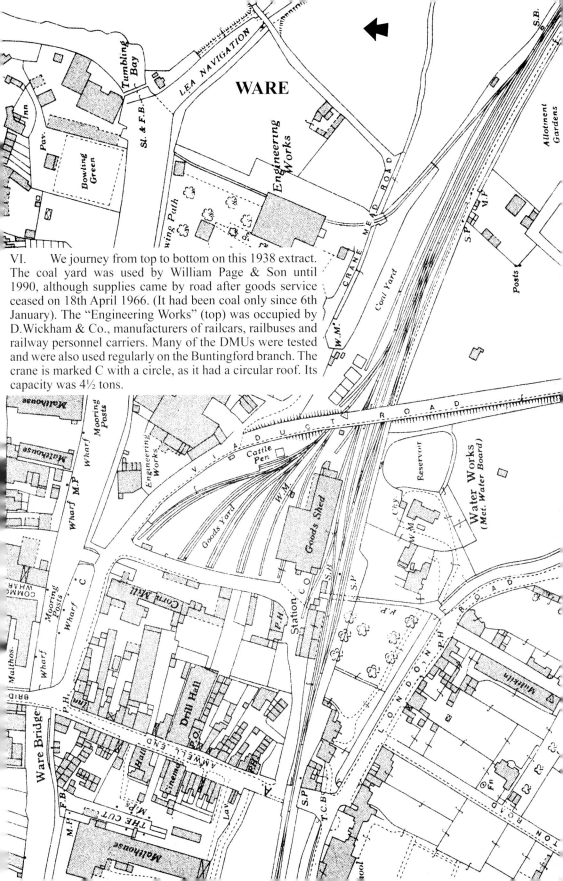

WARE

VI.   We journey from top to bottom on this 1938 extract. The coal yard was used by William Page & Son until 1990, although supplies came by road after goods service ceased on 18th April 1966. (It had been coal only since 6th January). The "Engineering Works" (top) was occupied by D.Wickham & Co., manufacturers of railcars, railbuses and railway personnel carriers. Many of the DMUs were tested and were also used regularly on the Buntingford branch. The crane is marked C with a circle, as it had a circular roof. Its capacity was 4½ tons.

19.   This is the north elevation and one of the GER poster boards is offering a Cook's Tour Round the World, while a choice of local road transport is on offer. (Lens of Sutton coll.)

20.   A view north up Amwell End includes the massive posts provided for the individual gates over the single line. The canal bridge is in the distance, with the town centre beyond. The population grew from 6456 in 1901 to 11,570 in 1961. (G.Woodward coll.)

21.	An early postcard includes the public footpath which bisected the site and was provided with a gas light. The point rods and signal wires run close to the path. (Lens of Sutton coll.)

22.	An eastward panorama in 1956 includes the convenient Station Hotel, which closed in 1993. The bridge carries Viaduct Road. The platform was extended in the distance at the time of electrification. (H.C.Casserley)

23.   A 1957 photograph includes the footpath and shows that it continued under the wagons on the right. The running lines become single in the foreground, owing to the New River Company refusing to part with land in the distance. The signal box had 33 levers and closed on 21st January 1961. The level crossing gates were operated manually at this time, with a gatekeeper based in a hut by the gates. (R.M.Casserley)

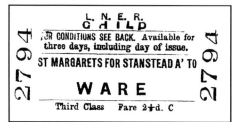

2794   2794

L. N. E. R.
CHILD
FOR CONDITIONS SEE BACK. Available for
three days, including day of issue.
ST MARGARETS FOR STANSTEAD A' TO
WARE
Third Class   Fare 2½d. C

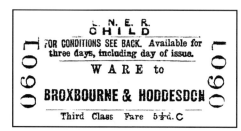

0601   0601

L. N. E. R.
CHILD
FOR CONDITIONS SEE BACK. Available for
three days, including day of issue.
WARE to
BROXBOURNE & HODDESDON
Third Class   Fare 5½d. C

24.   The 1959 footbridge is evident beyond the black panels of the signal box, as a train departs for Hertford on 7th May 1960. The panels acted as sun shades. (Milepost 92½)

25.   The footbridge is top left on the same day as an L1 2-6-4T runs in from Hertford East. The maltings in the background were destroyed by fire in 1986. The 20-lever signal box opened on 20th January 1960. (Milepost 92½)

26. The goods yard was provided with this small diesel shunter, which replaced an equally tiny North British Railway petrol-engined loco no. 68189. Seen on 3rd September 1960 is no. D2950. The yard was laid out on the site of the canal basin. (R.S.Carpenter)

27. The station survived demolition and is in the background as no. 315815 departs west on 17th November 1988. This class was introduced to the line in 1984. Note the unusual barriers. (D.Pollock)

28.   Modern styling and colour light signalling contrasted with rod worked points and a gas stove. The box closed on 18th May 2003, but was not demolished until January 2009. (D.Pollock)

B.P

L

S t

VII. The 1923 edition has our route from Ware on the right and the single line connection to the GNR on the left. The 1843 station was at the end of Railway Place and the 1888 terminus is in Railway Street; this one is still in use. The first building lasted into the 1960s and was adjacent to the goods shed. South of them was the Great Eastern Tavern, marked *Tav*. The tracks at the top of the right page served gravel pits. The present terminus became "Hertford East" on 1st July 1923. The crane shown was rated at four tons capacity. There are three signal boxes: "Junction" on the right, "Station" in the middle and "Dicker Mill" at Mill Road, for the level crossing. The gasworks had its own siding by 1927 and used 4987 tons of coal that year. Some may have still come on the River Lea. The area south of the lines on the inset diagram was used for coal storage, while the ground to the north took coke awaiting despatch. Production ceased in about 1957.

Dicker Mill
(Oilcake)

Tk.

Chy.

F.B.

Sluice

F.B.

Stant

R **D**

Columbia
Record

Leaside

Tks.

Chy.

GASHOUSE LANE

F.B.

Electricity
Works

F.P.

F.B.

SPENCER

STREET

BASIN

MILL ROAD

Crane

S.B.

S.P.

BRANCH

Corporation
Depôt

S.P.

S.P.

Saw Mill

TOWNSHEND

Station

R.C.
Chapel

Fire Eng.
Sta.

VILLIERS ST

ST JOHN'S STREET

Sch.

L.B.

RAILWAY STREET

Station
Hotel

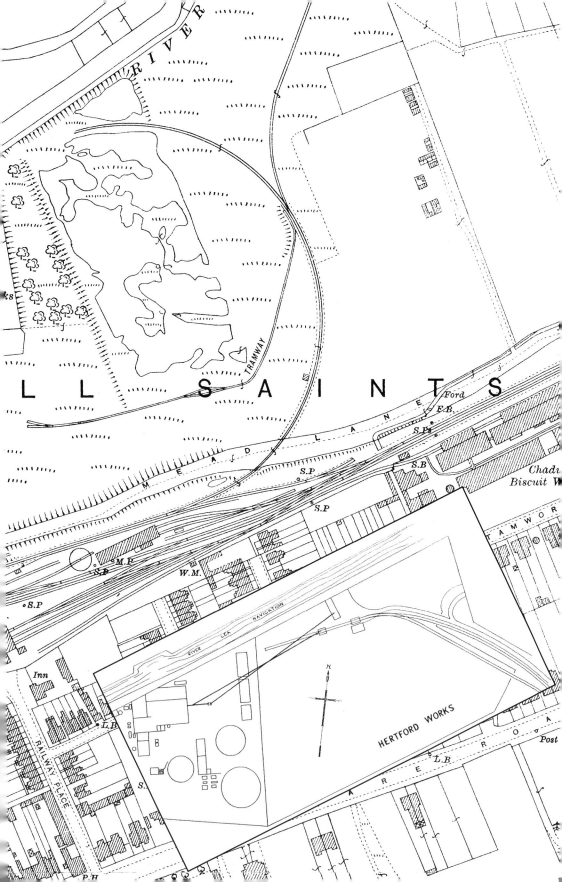

29.   An eastward panorama from about 1910 has the double track to the terminus in the foreground. The first engine shed had a single track and was in the area on the right. It had to be demolished in 1858 when the link to the GNR was built. This shed dates from that period and was extended eastwards in 1891-92. Junction Box is included, but this closed in 1925; it had 28 levers. (A.Dudman coll.)

30.   The growing town justified a prestigious station; the census showed 9322 residents in 1901 and 17,290 in 1961. This postcard includes the locomotive inspection pit and two six-wheelers for instant train lengthening. (Lens of Sutton coll.)

HERTFORD EAST

31.   Class N7 0-6-2T no. 69700 is about to use the crossover and engine release road sometime in the 1950s. The inspection pits had been infilled by that time and the length of the canopies was reduced during World War II. (Lens of Sutton coll.)

32.   Featured in June 1956 is a Quad Art set with only small gaps between the bodies. The term refers to four coaches articulated on five bogies, a system reinvented for Eurostar. The loading dock is visible on the left. (H.C.Casserley)

33.   When Junction Box closed, this box had its number of levers increased from 36 to 45 and its suffix was dropped. It is pictured on 16th July 1959, along with class J69/1 0-6-0T no. 68500, which was acting as a station pilot that day. The box was built in 1888 and closed on 18th May 2003. (J.Langford)

34.	The much altered engine shed is seen shortly before it was closed on 21st November 1960. In its final years it was coded 30B and usually had twelve locomotives allocated. (R.S.Carpenter)

35.	We look east from Mill Road along the single line goods connection in May 1961, with a DMU berthed on it. The cattle dock gates are on the left; its platform spans the join in the map. (Milepost 92½)

36.　　The fine architectural detail was recorded in the 1970s and all remains standing, having been listed Grade II. A similar station was built in Norwich. Extensive restoration work took place in 2000. The building had opened on 27th February 1888. (Lens of Sutton coll.)

37.　　A busy time was recorded on 18th November 1988 as no. 47316 awaits departure. It was booked to run Willesden Brent Sidings - Temple Mills Yard - Broxbourne - Hertford East - Broxbourne - Harlow Mill - Broxbourne Reception, then returning to Willesden Brent sidings via Temple Mills Yard. This was the last vestige of the pick up goods in the area and could often find itself extended down to Bishops Stortford if traffic warranted it. Booked to depart at 11.14, the wagons would be shunted in the Costain sidings at Rye House, where a loaded rake of wagons would be waiting for collection. Centre is 4 car EMU 315858 waiting departure with a Liverpool Street service, with 3-car EMU 305406 on the right, in the carriage sidings. (D.Pollock)

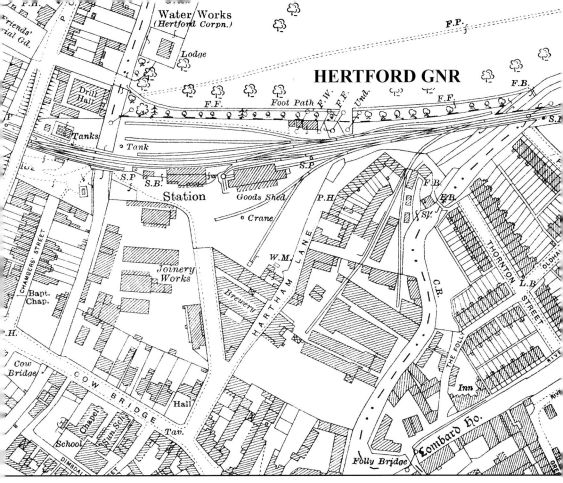

VIII.   The 1858 terminus for trains from Hatfield was well situated to the town centre and was often known as "Cowbridge"; the street and bridge are lower left. The bridge is over the River Beane. "North" was applied from 1st July 1923 until its closure on 2nd June 1924. Goods traffic continued until 18th April 1966, when the link to Hertford East also closed. The crane shown was listed as a 5-ton one in 1923, also the year of this survey.

38.   This is the well balanced south elevation, with the 30-lever signal box on the left. Passengers bound for London travelled via Hatfield and arrived at Kings Cross. (Lens of Sutton coll.)

39.   Another postcard and this also includes the signal box. There were three coal sidings adjacent to the run-round loop and the water tank is at the end of the nearest one. It was adjacent to the river. (Lens of Sutton coll.)

40.   A panorama in the other direction has the river across the middle, but the only evidence is the curved girders on the right. The goods shed is the large building on the left. The tallest building is the brewery, which was at the end of the goods yard. (Lens of Sutton coll.)

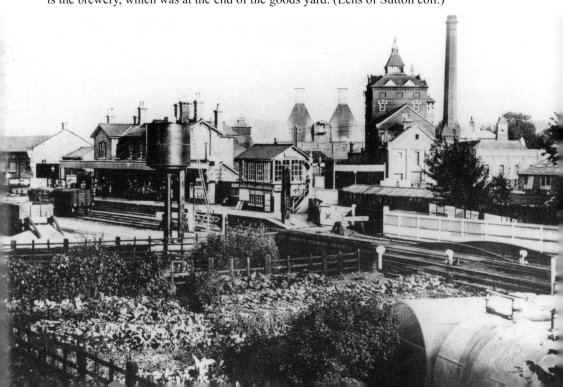

41.   The north elevation was photographed in November 1962. The canopy had long gone, but the spacious gents retained its generous ventilator and the goods shed was still intact. (E. Wilmshurst)

WEST OF HERTFORD

42.   Class N7/1 0-6-2T no. 69637 approaches the new Hertford North on 18th October 1952, with freight from Hertford East. It has just passed over North Road bridge. This section of route was always single. (P.J. Kelley)

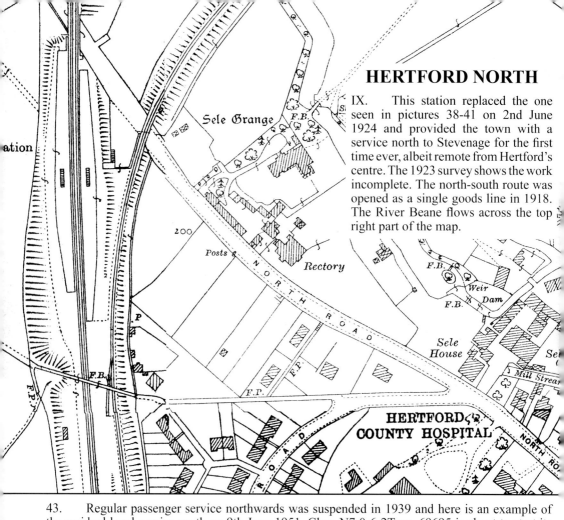

HERTFORD NORTH

IX.   This station replaced the one seen in pictures 38-41 on 2nd June 1924 and provided the town with a service north to Stevenage for the first time ever, albeit remote from Hertford's centre. The 1923 survey shows the work incomplete. The north-south route was opened as a single goods line in 1918. The River Beane flows across the top right part of the map.

43.   Regular passenger service northwards was suspended in 1939 and here is an example of the residual local service south on 9th June 1951. Class N7 0-6-2T no. 69695 is about to start its journey to Welwyn Garden City at 5.45pm. (R.F.Roberts/SLS coll.)

44.   No. 69695 arrives earlier on the same day with empty stock and is about to take water. The line on the right serves the down bay; the up one never received track. The bridge was provided for a public footpath and beyond it was the junction for Hatfield. (R.F.Roberts/SLS coll.)

45.   The coal is trimmed while class N2 0-6-2T no. 69572 waits in the bay to return south at 1.31pm on 20th September 1958. The locomotive was built by Hawthorn Leslie and was in use from December 1928 until February 1961. (F.Hornby)

46.   The service north to Stevenage was restored on 5th March 1962 and we see a DMU on that route on 4th May 1969. The trackbed of the original route to Hertford North curves above the right hand light. The down bay and its run-round loop is included. (R.Hummerston)

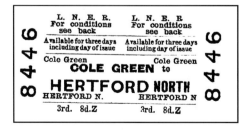

SOUTH OF HERTFORD NORTH

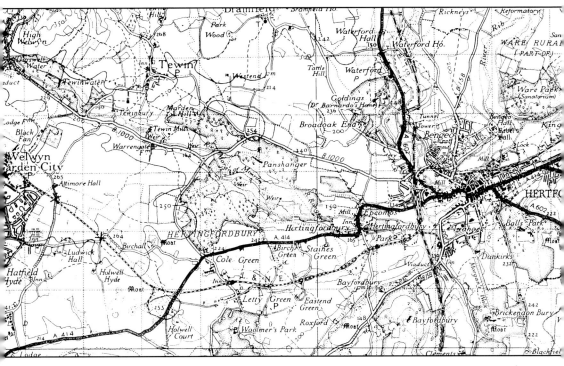

X.   The 1945 map at 1ins to 1 mile has the 1858 route across it. There were short-lived halts in 1904-05 on the left at Attimore Hall and Hatfield Hyde. Both were near the level crossings, which are marked X.

47.   The 1858 route is in the foreground and the connection between it and the 1918 lines is on the left, largely obscured by grass in this southward view. These lines are known as the Hertford Loop and were electrified in 1976 south from here and in 1978 northwards. (Milepost 92½)

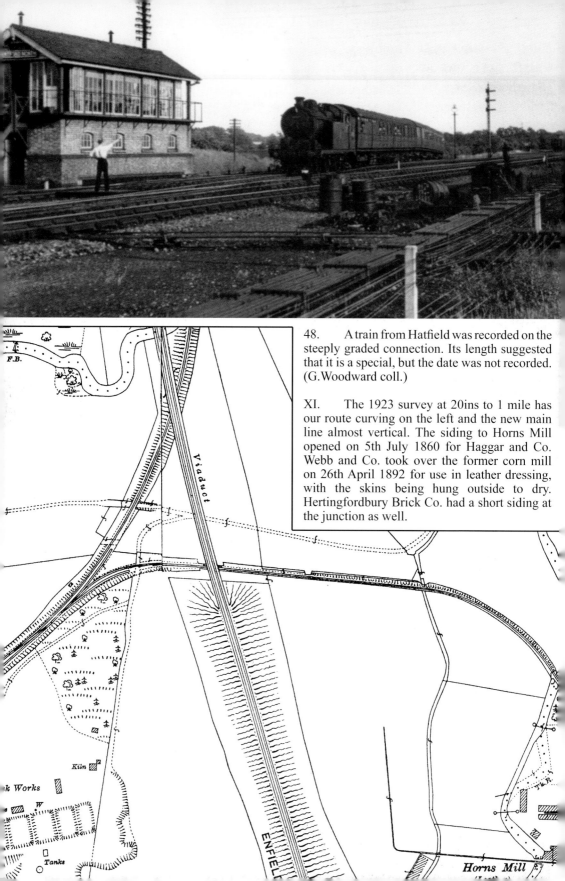

48. A train from Hatfield was recorded on the steeply graded connection. Its length suggested that it is a special, but the date was not recorded. (G. Woodward coll.)

XI. The 1923 survey at 20ins to 1 mile has our route curving on the left and the new main line almost vertical. The siding to Horns Mill opened on 5th July 1860 for Haggar and Co. Webb and Co. took over the former corn mill on 26th April 1892 for use in leather dressing, with the skins being hung outside to dry. Hertingfordbury Brick Co. had a short siding at the junction as well.

49. Class N1 0-6-2T no. 69484 is bound for Hatfield in 1951 and is passing under Hertford Viaduct, which carries the Hertford Loop. The large pipe is for condensing exhaust steam when working underground in London. (R.F.Roberts/SLS coll.)

50. Webb's siding was photographed in the 1950s, while a goods train passes over the viaduct. This is on the left of the map. The points for the mill siding are just beyond the rear wagon. (Views of Wells)

HERTINGFORDBURY

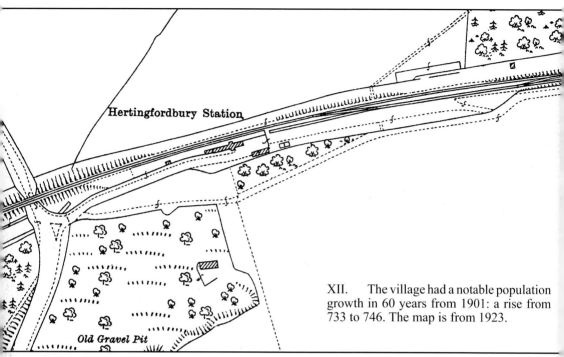

Hertingfordbury Station

Old Gravel Pit

XII.   The village had a notable population growth in 60 years from 1901: a rise from 733 to 746. The map is from 1923.

51.   A close-up view after passenger closure includes the loading gauge in the goods yard, which ceased to be used on 5th March 1962. Oil lighting was in use to the end. (G.Woodward coll.)

52.   The station approach and the entrance to the goods yard were recorded in September 1962. The village was within ½ mile of the station, to the north of it. (R.M.Casserley)

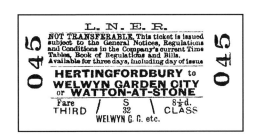

COLE GREEN

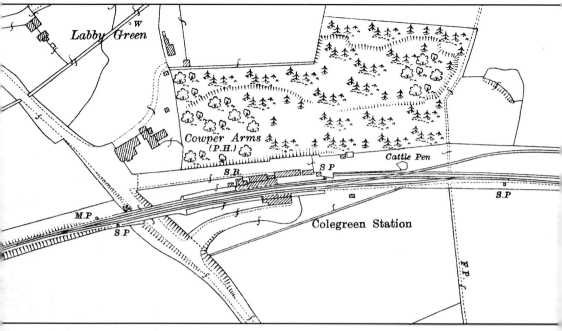

XIII. The 1923 map includes the two sidings, which were in use until 1st August 1962.

53.   An eastward view in June 1951 features the surprisingly large canopy, under which is the signal box, at the far end. Its 30-lever frame was used from 1st July 1891 until 1st September 1951, when it became a ground frame. There was no habitation nearby, the tiny village being scattered to the north. (G.Woodward coll.)

54. November 1959 and a railtour appeared. The Cravens 2-car DMU has the destination KINGS CROSS. (G.Woodward coll.)

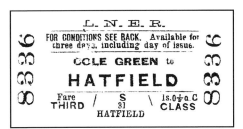

NORTH OF WELWYN GARDEN CITY

55.   This northward panorama is from the approach to the bridge north of the present station and includes the staff platform on the single line from Hertford. Although not visible, this curves away from the main line in the distance. A connection from the down slow line to the Hertford route was added on 17th September 1944. Passenger trains to Dunstable used the curve on the left until withdrawn in 1965. There was a platform on it for workers in 1920-26.
(D.White/G.Woodward coll.)

56.   Refuse trains started running to Holwell Hyde sandpits in about 1935 for infilling with London refuse. This traffic ceased on 23rd May 1966 and the line was cut back to the site of Attimore Halt, which was near the gates in the background. The line served private sidings until 16th November 1981. The end is seen in 1968. (R.Hummerston)

WELWYN GARDEN CITY

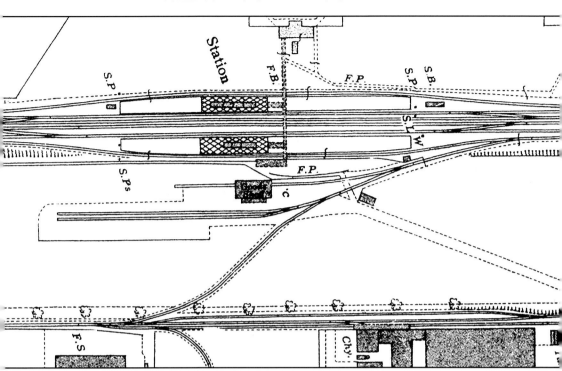

XIV.   An extensive housing and industrial development was begun in the early 1920s and a station with four platforms was opened on 20th September 1926. Its plan is shown on the 1937 edition, together with two of several private sidings at the bottom. The goods yard had been completed by 1932.

57.   Most trains from Hertford North terminated here instead of Hatfield from 17th September 1944. This one was hauled by class N7 no. 69640 on 1st June 1951 and is ready to return to Hertford. (R.F.Roberts/SLS)

58.   Period costume was worn by some on the last day of operation of Hertford trains, 16th June 1951. Class N7 no. 69695 worked the final trip, the 7.18pm from Hertford North. (R.F.Roberts/SLS)

59.   North of the road bridge, on the down side, nine berthing sidings were created in association with the electrification in 1988. There were also eight other sidings on the up side. A flyover was built in 1987, in the distance, for use by trains terminating at platform 4, right. This southward panorama is from 1956. (H.C.Casserley)

60.	Notable features east of the platforms are the goods shed and the 1925 Shredded Wheat factory. The latter is shown lower right on the map. A massive marshalling yard south of them was begun in 1944, this being intended to reduce congestion at Hatfield. (Lens of Sutton coll.)

Other views of this station can be seen in pictures 23 to 29 in the *Potters Bar to Cambridge* album and nos 108 to 111 in *Branch Line to Dunstable.*

61.	A view south from the Bridge Road bridge in 1969 includes the station building, partially hidden in the woods. New multi-storey facilities replaced it in 1990. The signal box lasted until 26th September 1976. (G.Woodward coll.)

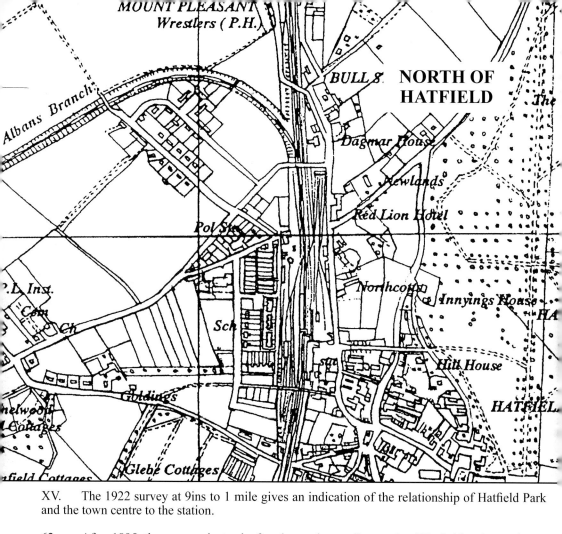

Map labels (as they appear):

MOUNT PLEASANT
Wrestlers (P.H.)

Albans Branch

BULL S NORTH OF
HATFIELD

The

Dagmar House

Newlands

Red Lion Hotel

Pol Sta

P.L. Inst.

Com

Ch

Northcott

Innyings House

HA

Sch

Hill House

Goldings

HATFIEL

nelwood
Cottages

Glebe Cottages

afield Cottages

XV.   The 1922 survey at 9ins to 1 mile gives an indication of the relationship of Hatfield Park and the town centre to the station.

62.   After 1895, there were six tracks for almost three miles north of Hatfield and we witness freight southbound on the Hertford line. On the left is the single line used by Dunstable trains in both directions. (G.Woodward coll.)

63.   Running from Hertford sometime in 1937 is class N5 0-6-2T no. 5535. Note the articulated stock with only three bogies for two coaches. (G.Woodward coll.)

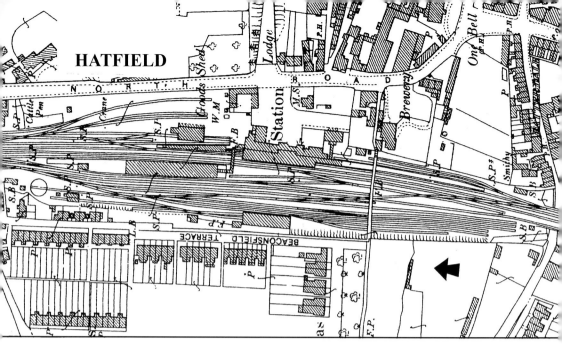

HATFIELD

XVI.   The 1898 survey is included at 20ins to 1 mile to show all three signal boxes. The cramped layout of the marshalling yard (lower right) is evident. The loco depot is lower left and the goods yard is upper left. There appears to be a down island platform, but its western face served as a bay for both Dunstable and St. Albans trains; sometimes both at once. In 1941, a direct connection from the down slow line was provided on the right. The gas company was formed in 1860 and it had its own wagons, but not a siding. In 1917, 1670 tons of coal was carted by road from the goods yard, the figure rising to 6270 in 1927, when the Welwyn Gas Co. took over. Production ceased in 1932.

64.   The bridge at the south end of the station carried a public footpath and was not used by passengers. The rear of this up train is under an extension of the canopy, which is supported by ten stanchions. (R.M.Casserley coll.)

65.   One of the roof stanchions is on the left of this record of the up platform. The supports were soon to be lost. Gas lighting was provided from an early date, the works being close to the station. (Lens of Sutton coll.)

66.   Private owner coal wagons and loaded cattle trucks create a period atmosphere in this 1930s northward view, in which the engine number appears to be 4534, an ex-GNR class C12. The map does not show loco shed access from the south. (Lens of Sutton coll.)

67.   We can now enjoy two photographs from 11th August 1945. To the right of the horse box is the track to the Hertford bay platform in which two vans stand. Less clear at the far end of the up platform is another bay, which was used by London stopping trains. (H.C.Casserley)

68.   Class N2 0-6-2T no. 4747 is standing north of the engine shed, alongside the narrow gauge coaling tubs. The diagonal white line indicates which end of the wagon opens. (H.C.Casserley)

69.　　Sherriff's private siding was north of the station and it is seen on 28th September 1946 showing its new LNER number. It is an ex-GER class J69. Sherriff's Granary was built in 1899 alongside the Great North Road and was served by a siding from the up goods yard. It was demolished in 1987 for redevelopment. (H.C.Casserley)

70.　　Standing at platform 4 on 28th September 1951 is class N7 0-6-2T no. 69644 with the 5.8pm to St. Albans, the last advertised service. (P.J.Kelley)

71.   The engine shed has been reroofed since we last saw it and the N7 is bearing the destination board for MOORGATE, suitably inverted to indicate that it is going nowhere. The date is 23rd May 1959; the shed closed on 2nd January 1961. (F.Hornby)

72.   Little remained of the Hertford bay before the station was totally rebuilt in 1972. General goods traffic ceased on 7th January 1980. Three through platforms continued to be available, but the up bay was lost. (G.Woodward coll.)

73.   A northward panorama from the bridge seen in the previous picture includes two signal boxes in August 1969. No. 2 Box is on the right of the main lines, its 85-lever frame being in use until 20th May 1973. It had a panel from then until closure on 3rd March 1974. Part of No. 3 Box is evident on the left. Its 80-lever frame served until 30th November 1969. No. 1 Box was south of the station. It had 60 levers and lasted until 20th May 1973. (G.Woodward coll.)

Other illustrations of these locations can be seen in photographs 112 to 120 in *Branch Line to Dunstable* and nos. 15 to 22 in *Potters Bar to Cambridge*.

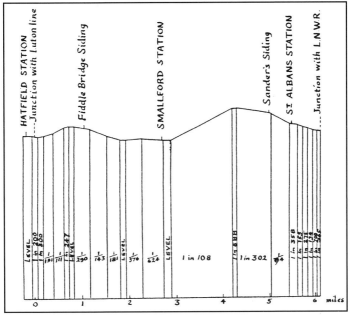

Branch gradient profile.

NAST HYDE HALT

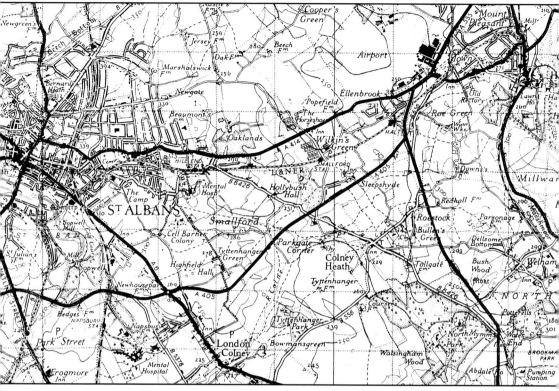

XVII. The 1945 edition at 1ins to 1 mile shows the massive de Havilland aircraft factory in black, to the right of the word "Airport". Below "New Town" was Fiddle Bridge Siding and Lemsford Road Halt, both primarily serving the works. The latter opened on 1st August 1942, but did not appear in timetables. The siding was provided in about 1880 for manure traffic.

74.   Nast Hyde Halt was almost two miles from Hatfield station and is near the convergence of the three main roads shown west of the town. It was opened on 1st February 1910, near the level crossing. The house for the crossing keeper can be seen beyond the waiting shelter, which was photographed in 1962. (S.F.Page)

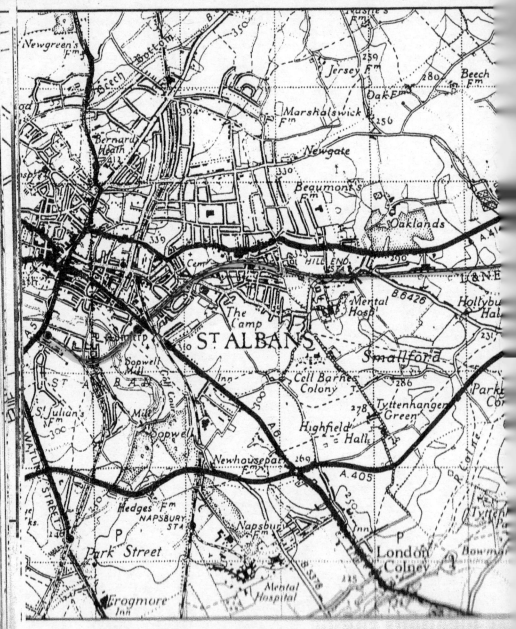

XVII. The 1945 edition at 1 ins to 1 mile shows th
to the right of the word "Airport". Below "New I
Road Halt, both primarily serving the works. The
appear in timetables. The siding was provided in a

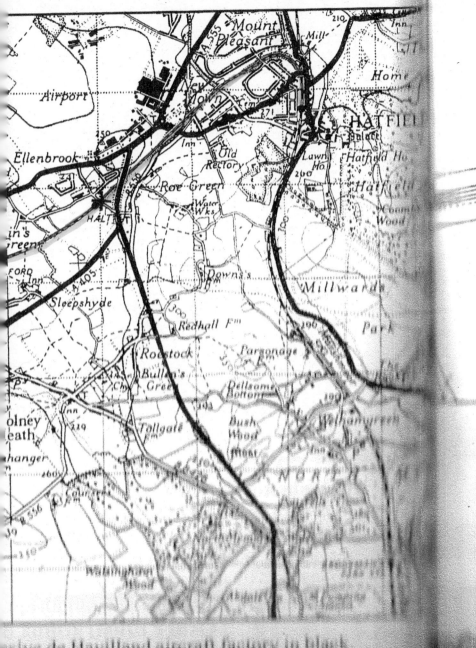

...sive de Havilland aircraft factory in black.
...? was Fiddle Bridge Siding and Lemsford
...r opened on 1st August 1942, but did not
...1880 for manure traffic.

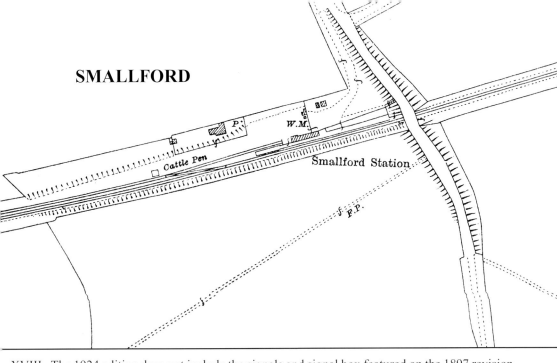

SMALLFORD

P.

W.M.

Cattle Pen

Smallford Station

F.P.

XVIII. The 1924 edition does not include the signals and signal box featured on the 1897 revision. The site was used by a scrap metal merchant E. Pearce & Sons after line closure.

75.   Ex-GNR 0-6-0T no. 1247 became no. 68846 and was restored to its original form to be photographed with brake vans packed with enthusiasts on 17th June 1961. It was normally kept in Mowlem's Yard at Marshmoor, south of Hatfield and was one of the first privately preserved locomotives to run on BR. (P.J.Kelley)

76.   This view towards Hatfield is from April 1967, when coal still came by rail to the yard. All goods traffic ceased when the route closed on 1st January 1969. The building was used for ladies hairdressing for a period after 1951. (R.Hummerston)

77.   The prospective passenger's perspective was recorded belatedly on 17th September 1974. The station had opened in May 1866 and was known as "Springfield" until 1st October 1879. An emergency food store opened west of the station in 1941 and was served by Butterwick Sidings. A banana warehouse was added later and traffic continued until line closure. (R.M.Casserley)

HILL END

78.   A siding was provided here in about 1895 during the building of the Herts County Mental Hospital and its station opened officially on 1st August 1899. It is seen in July 1958, following fire damage earlier. (J.Langford)

XIX.   The 1924 edition at 20ins to 1 mile has the line to the hospital crossing the road. It was used mainly for coal for the boilers, but latterly oil. A siding for Owen's brickworks existed from about 1899 to 1940 and is on the left. Further west was Fleetville siding from about 1905 and it served the printing works of Orford Smith, which had moved from Fleet Street.

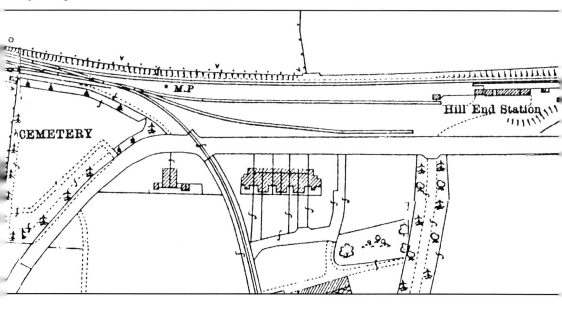

SALVATION ARMY HALT

79.   The Salvation Army Printing Works opened in 1901 and 15 to 20 tons of *The War Cry* were despatched weekly. It became known as Campfield Press. Brass band instruments were also produced in the works. The staff platform is seen in 1958. (J.Langford)

XX.   The short siding on the left of this 1924 map was added in 1890 for orchid transport and special ventilated vans were provided by the GNR. The traffic ceased by 1939. The siding is in the background of the picture. The halt was used by the public in 1929-42; it is shown as a line lower left.

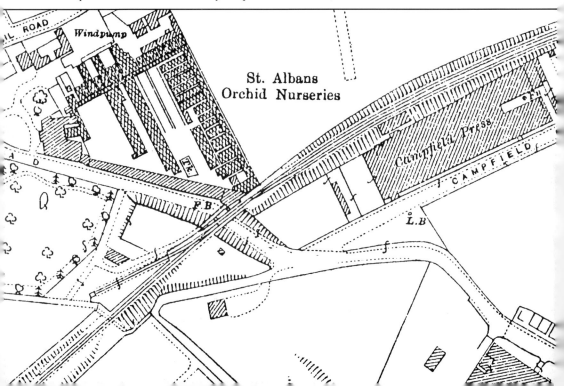

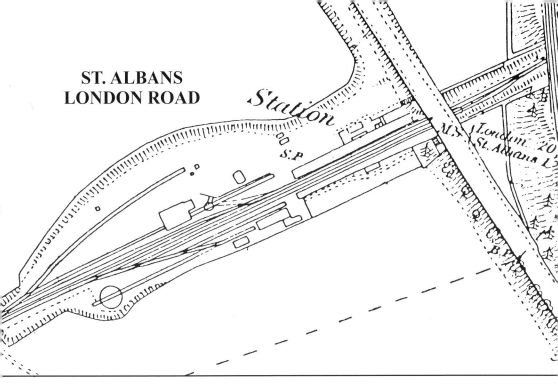

ST. ALBANS
LONDON ROAD

XXI.   The 1872 survey indicates that the engine shed had lost its track by that time, but that the 45ft turntable was still in place, as was the run-round loop. Note the wagon turntable near the end-loading dock. The MR of 1868 is on the right, but was never connected owing to a great height difference. The footpath lower left had been London Road until 1793.

80.   A 1954 eastward view has the remains of the down platform and the loop on the right. The lower bridge carries London Road (then the A6), the higher one having been built for the MR. There was a staff of 17 in 1920. (H.C.Casserley)

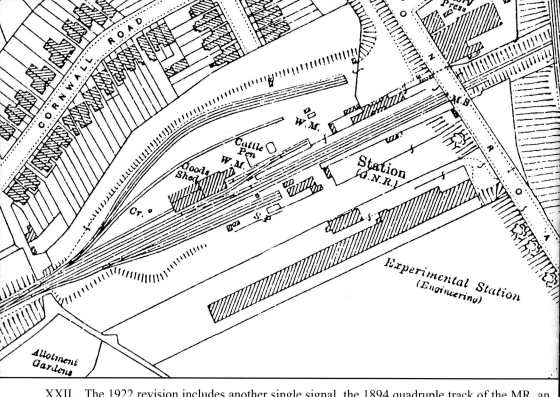

XXII. The 1922 revision includes another single signal, the 1894 quadruple track of the MR, an extended goods shed, a curtailed loop and a crane (Cr.), which was rated at 5 tons.

81. The engine shed was still standing more than 80 years after it had closed. It was more convenient to supply locomotives for the branch from Hatfield shed. The building was used as stables for many years, for the railway's horses. (R.M.Casserley coll.)

82.   It is July 1958 and the coaches on the left are for engineering staff. There had been a small signal box on the left, which acted as a block post until about 1915. A few trains from Hatfield terminated here until that time: 3 in 1869, 1 in 1889 and 2 in 1909 for example. The goods yard closed on 5th October 1964. (B.Leslie)

83.   The final view is also from 1958. Widely known as London Road, the station appeared in timetables and other documents as GNR, LNER and finally ER. (D.K.Jones coll.)

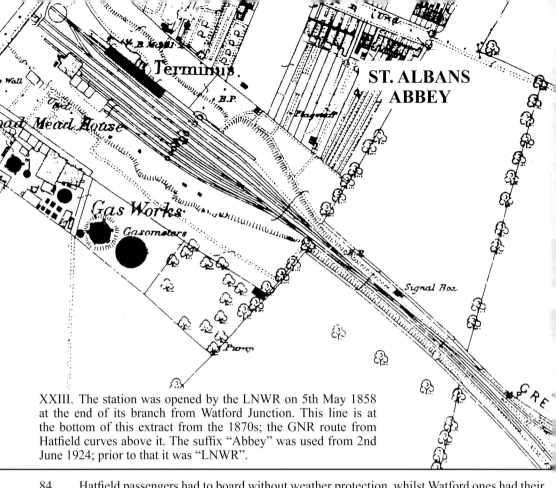

ST. ALBANS
ABBEY

XXIII. The station was opened by the LNWR on 5th May 1858 at the end of its branch from Watford Junction. This line is at the bottom of this extract from the 1870s; the GNR route from Hatfield curves above it. The suffix "Abbey" was used from 2nd June 1924; prior to that it was "LNWR".

84.   Hatfield passengers had to board without weather protection, whilst Watford ones had their platform and train in the dry. Class N7 0-6-2T no. 2651 is seen in about 1930; it was renumbered 9691 in the late 1940s. (R.M.Casserley coll.)

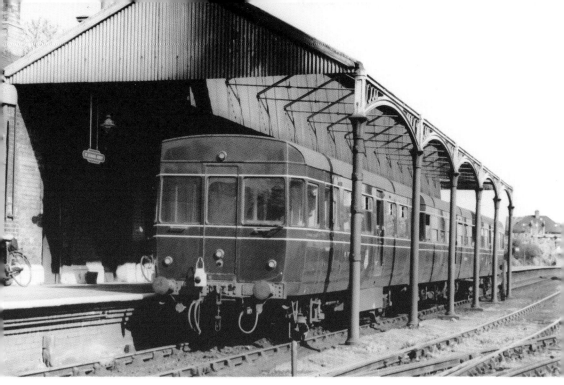

85.	British United Traction supplied two 3-car DMUs for the Watford service in July 1955 and one is seen soon after. AC Cars had provided other units in 1952. The glass had gone and iron sheets sheltered just the platform. (M.J.Stretton coll.)

The branch from Watford is included with three others in our *Harrow to Watford* album. The MR line is in *St. Pancras to St. Albans* and *St. Albans to Bedford*.

86.	On 30th April 1955, the RCTS ran a railtour which had class B16 4-6-0 from St. Pancras and it ran via Tottenham South Junction and Ware to Hatfield. Ex-GNR class J52 0-6-0ST no. 68878 ran from there and an ex-LNWR 0-8-0 returned the train to St. Pancras. (D.T.Rowe)

87.   On the left are some of the buildings of the gasworks, which was opened in 1836 and received coal direct by rail from 1858 until 1971. The tank wagons probably contain tar or other liquors from it. A road van is loaded on the right of this 1957 photograph. (D.K.Jones coll.)

88.   The RCTS ran a railtour on 27th April 1958 using ex-LMS 0-4-4T no. 41901. A van body had formed extra storage space for many years. Freight traffic ceased on 5th October 1964. (M.J.Stretton coll.)

89. The convergence of the routes is near the signal box, the track on the left being just a siding. The signal box had 25 levers and was in use until 7th August 1966. (G.Woodward coll.)

90. The station was built and owned by the LNWR and the bay on the left was added in about 1900. Staffing ceased on 16th January 1966 and fares were subsequently collected on the trains, which have been electrically operated since 11th July 1988. An extension to the gas works is in progress on the right in April 1958. (B.Leslie)

Buntingford Branch
WEST OF ST. MARGARET'S

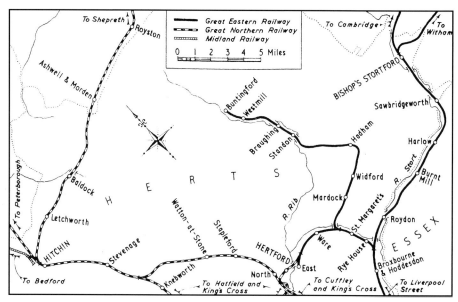

XXIV. Nearly one mile west of St. Margaret's, the branch curved away northwards from the Hertford line. This diagram shows the pre-1923 ownerships. (Railway Magazine)

→ 91. The divergence of the lines was recorded from a DMU in 1963. The third track was retained this far until 1969, for possible use as a ballast siding. The line northwards was soon lifted and the trackbed became the Amwell Walkway. (D.W.Sharp)

Branch gradient profile.

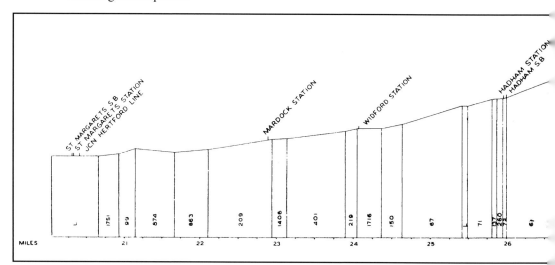

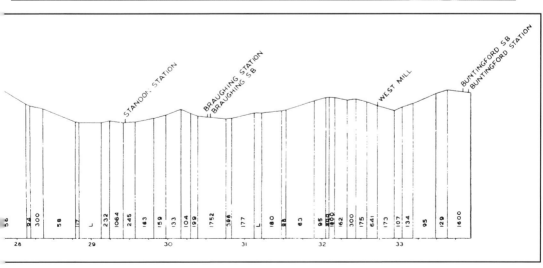

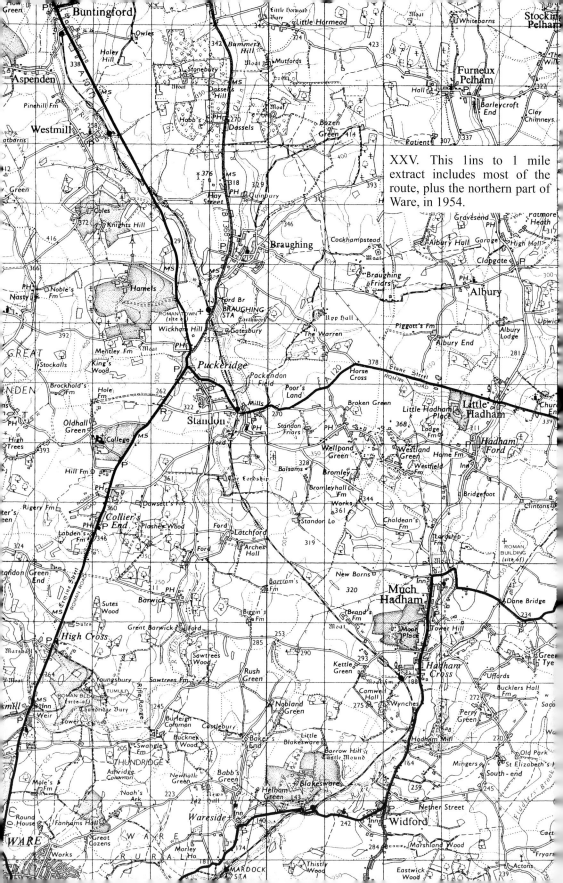

XXV. This 1ins to 1 mile extract includes most of the route, plus the northern part of Ware, in 1954.

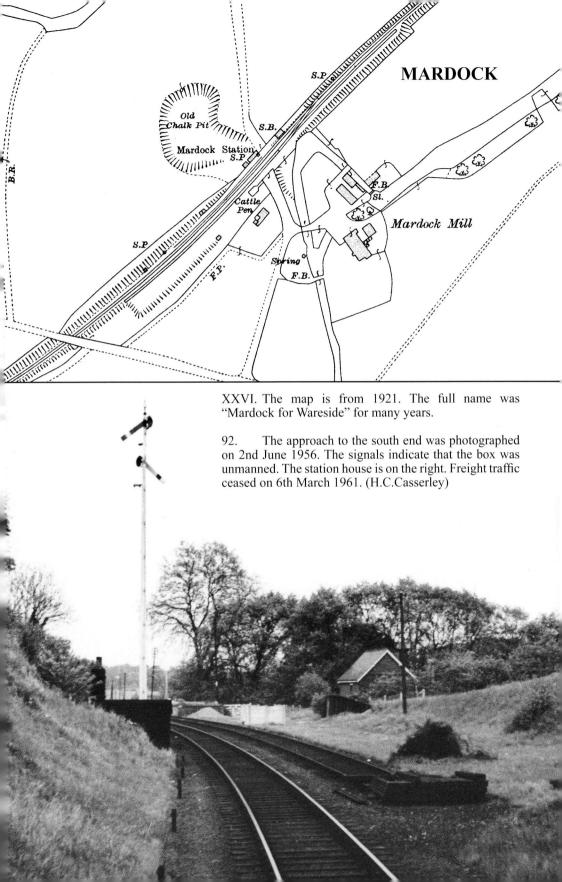

MARDOCK

XXVI. The map is from 1921. The full name was "Mardock for Wareside" for many years.

92.	The approach to the south end was photographed on 2nd June 1956. The signals indicate that the box was unmanned. The station house is on the right. Freight traffic ceased on 6th March 1961. (H.C.Casserley)

93.   Seen on the same day is the solitary employee. He had no water supply, but it could be obtained from the river by the tree, on the right. The signal box had 15 levers and closed on 1st April 1962. (H.C.Casserley)

94.   Some original buildings of the WHBR remained here, on the right. The one with a pitched roof was a waiting room of later addition. The road led to Mardock Farm only. The siding was removed in 1962. (Lens of Sutton coll.)

WIDFORD

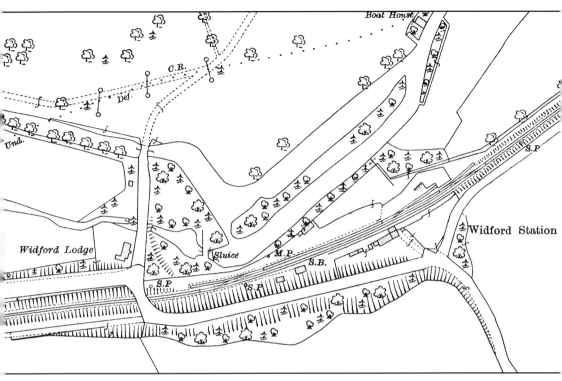

XXVII. Again the map is from 1921 and the station is very close to the river. We travel from left to right.

95.   The population was 456 in 1861 and 402 in 1961. The revenue was so poor that the station was closed for the first three months of 1869. (Lens of Sutton coll.)

96. Facilities were provided for gentlemen (left) and these included a flush toilet, as the station had a well as its water source. (Lens of Sutton coll.)

→ 97. The signal box had 15 operational levers, the building being disproportionate to its task. It was only used during shunting and all goods traffic ceased on 7th September 1964. (Lens of Sutton coll.)

→ 98. The cattle dock (left) was added in August 1896, but otherwise little changed. DMUs were introduced on the branch in June 1959 and this example is seen on the last day of operation, 14th November 1964. The sign declares WIDFORD FOR HUNSDON. (H.Ballantyne)

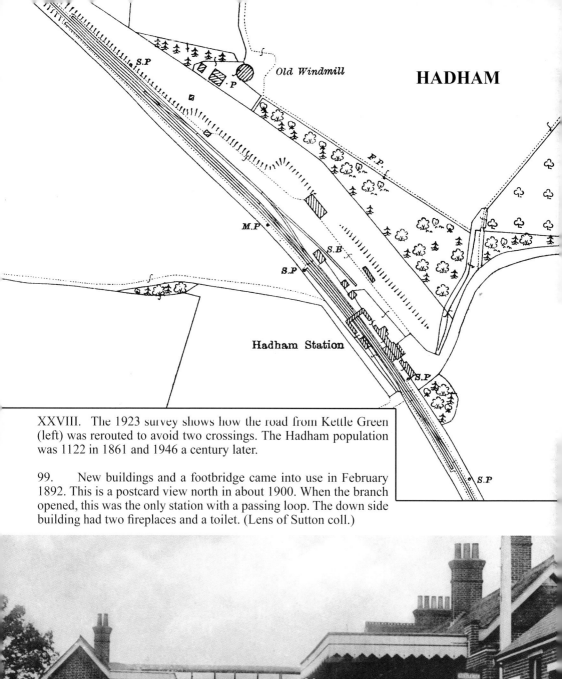

HADHAM

Old Windmill

S.P

.P

M.P

S.B

S.P

Hadham Station

S.P

S.P

XXVIII. The 1923 survey shows how the road from Kettle Green (left) was rerouted to avoid two crossings. The Hadham population was 1122 in 1861 and 1946 a century later.

99. New buildings and a footbridge came into use in February 1892. This is a postcard view north in about 1900. When the branch opened, this was the only station with a passing loop. The down side building had two fireplaces and a toilet. (Lens of Sutton coll.)

100. The station master was provided with a spacious house, with multiple chimneys, a large garden and a separate office (left). This and the next two views are from June 1956.
(H.C.Casserley)

101. Gas lighting was provided by the Much Hadham Gas Company in 1880, but this was changed to Tilley lamps not long before closure. The signal box had 27 levers and was in use until 24th December 1964.
(H.C.Casserley)

102. The footbridge and down shelter canopy were both lost in the 1930s. The 2.28pm from St. Margaret's was worked by no. 69685 on 2nd June 1956. The goods yard was in use to the end.
(H.C.Casserley)

STANDON

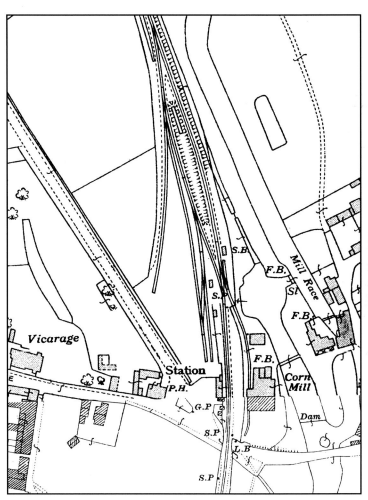

XXIX. The 1938 edition features the mill, which had a private siding from 1902 to the end. Nearby is the centre of Standon, which had developed from a medieval market town. The population was still under 3000 when the line closed.

103. The first station was of the type seen in picture 94, but it burnt down on 29th October 1867 and was replaced with this structure. On the right is a supplementary parcels shed, formed of a van body. (Lens of Sutton coll.)

104.   A northward panorama from the top of the mill in about 1905 reveals that the west siding was used for coal traffic. There is a branch from the mill siding, not shown on the map. The latter was used by British Soya Products in the final years of the branch, until its closure. (Views of Wells)

105.   In the background is the 20-lever signal box. A ground frame sufficed from January 1961. The station was electrically lit from 1911, the current being initially supplied by the nearby mill. This photograph is from around 1960. (Lens of Sutton coll.)

BRAUGHING

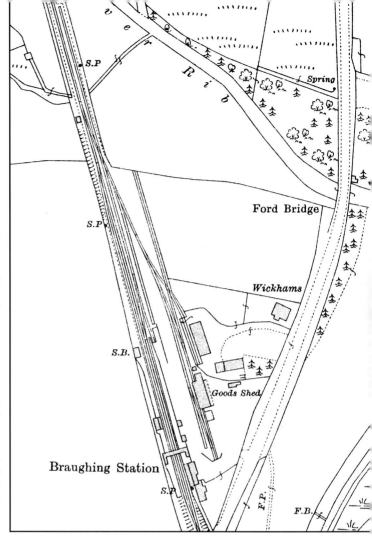

XXX. The station was ¾ mile south of the town, which had 1180 residents in 1861 and only 920 in 1961. The name is usually spoken as "Braffing". This is the 1921 layout.

106. The 1893 foot-bridge lasted into the 1930s. Behind the fence is a footpath, which saved passengers from the south having to walk to the main gate. Most trains were locomotive hauled, but there was some push-pull working from 1939.
(Lens of Sutton coll.)

107.   The station was renamed "Rathbarney" for the duration of Sunday 6th September 1953, for filming *O'Leary Night*. Some local stock was repainted in CIE livery. (P.J.Kelley)

108.   The loop and second platform came into use in August 1892. The waiting room on the right was identical to the one at Hadham; here we see the chimney stack. The parcels shed is opposite. (Lens of Sutton coll.)

109.   This northward view is from June 1956 and includes another example of an office for the station master. The signal box had 24 levers and closed on 24th December 1964. Watercress was despatched regularly to London from here until the late 1940s. (H.C.Casserley)

110.   The main building was photographed ten years after the last ticket was sold and it seemed in good order, apart from a blocked downpipe. (R.M.Casserley)

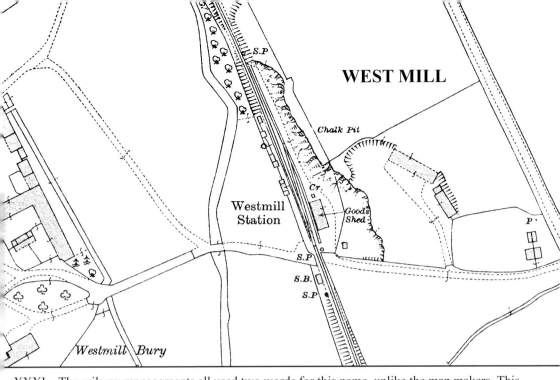

XXXI. The railway managements all used two words for this name, unlike the map makers. This is the 1921 edition. The "Goods Shed" is shown as a granary on other plans and it had vanished by 1939. It was privately owned.

111. A 1956 northward view includes the small booking office, which had an open waiting area behind the tiny canopy. A signal box is shown on the map, but it was demolished in 1936 and replaced by a 5-lever ground frame. The box had 16 levers. The station was used for Spike Milligan's film *Postman's Knock* in 1961. (H.C.Casserley)

112.　Looking south, we see another of the small offices, but this one is complete with its chimney. It seems that it was used as a waiting room for some time. Goods traffic ceased on 7th September 1964. The gates appear to have elevated targets. (A.Dudman coll.)

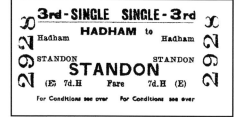

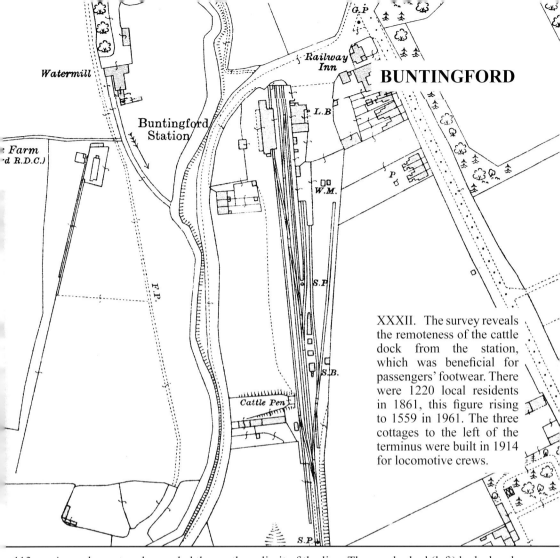

Watermill

Buntingford
Station

Farm
d R.D.C.)

G. P

Railway
Inn

BUNTINGFORD

L.B

W.M.

P

F.P.

S.P.

S.B.

Cattle Pen

XXXII. The survey reveals the remoteness of the cattle dock from the station, which was beneficial for passengers' footwear. There were 1220 local residents in 1861, this figure rising to 1559 in 1961. The three cottages to the left of the terminus were built in 1914 for locomotive crews.

S.P.

113. An early postcard recorded the northern limit of the line. The goods shed (left) had a hand-worked crane capable of lifting 30cwt. (Lens of Sutton coll.)

114.   An equally old card recorded the approach, together with the parcel delivery facility. There was also a horse-drawn cart until 1921. The left part formed the dwelling for the stationmaster. (Lens of Sutton coll.)

115.   A through train from Liverpool Street (at 6.0pm) was introduced on 10th July 1922 and it ran until 6th June 1953. A through coach in the reverse direction at 8.51am began on 11th September 1939 and more such departures were added after the war. This undated view has class F6 2-4-2T no. 7002 ready to depart. Classes F4 and F5 were also used regularly. (Milepost 92½)

116.   The 1.30pm from St. Margaret's has just arrived on 2nd June 1956, behind class N7/3 0-6-2T no. 69682. This type was introduced in 1943. Class N7s dominated branch traffic from 1950, following the electrification of the Shenfield route. (H.C.Casserley)

117.   No. 69634 was class N7/1, a type dating from 1925. It is running round on 16th April 1957, as we gain a glimpse of the cattle dock. There was a turntable nearby until about 1880. Extra traffic came during World War II, as there was a tank repair depot nearby. (R.M.Casserley coll.)

118.   No engine shed was provided, but a crew mess room was built between the water tank and the coal stage. The photograph is from 3rd September 1960. The last freight left on 17th September 1965. (R.S.Carpenter)

119.   Type 1 BTH/Paxman diesels were used on freight services after steam on the branch ceased on 18th November 1960. However, this one is hauling a RCTS railtour on 6th October 1962. It is no. D8236. The signal box had 28 levers and functioned until 24th December 1964. (Lens of Sutton coll.)

120.   The introduction of DMUs on 15th June 1959 brought through working, and also 1st class, to an end. The 9.55am departure was recorded on the last day of service, 14th November 1964. A notable century had just been exceeded. (H.Ballantyne)

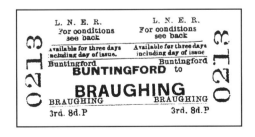

MP Middleton Press

EVOLVING THE ULTIMATE RAIL ENCYCLOPEDIA

Easebourne Lane, Midhurst, West Sussex.
GU29 9AZ   Tel:01730 813169

www.middletonpress.co.uk   email:info@middletonpress.co.uk

A-978 0 906520   B- 978 1 873793   C- 978 1 901706   D-978 1 904474   E - 978 1 906008

OOP Out of print at time of printing - Please check availability   BROCHURE AVAILABLE SHOWING NEW TITLES